BRAIN GAMES®

FIND THE CAT

pil

Publications International, Ltd.

Let's get social!

 @Publications_International

 @PublicationsInternational

 @BrainGames.TM

www.pilbooks.com

Here, Kitty, Kitty

Ready for a unique, picture-based puzzle book filled with furtive felines? This book contains cats that have snuck into the scene, and your job is to find them. Each picture has a single kitty. You'll have to carefully scan the scene because cats can hide just about anywhere, and the puzzles get more difficult as the book progresses. It's fun to search for these furry friends, and it's also good for your brain. A little mental stimulation every day helps you keep your cognitive abilities sharp. If you get stumped, you can always peek at the answers at the back of the book.

Answer on page 308.

Answer on page 308.

Answer on page 308.

Answer on page 308.

Answer on page 309.

Answer on page 309.

Answer on page 309.

Answer on page 309.

Answer on page 310.

Answer on page 310.

Answer on page 310.

Answer on page 310.

Answer on page 311.

Answer on page 311.

Answer on page 311.

Answer on page 311.

Answer on page 312.

Answer on page 312.

Answer on page 312.

Answer on page 312.

Answer on page 313.

Answer on page 313.

Answer on page 313.

Answer on page 313.

Answer on page 314.

Answer on page 314.

Answer on page 314.

Answer on page 314.

Answer on page 315.

Answer on page 315.

Answer on page 315.

Answer on page 315.

Answer on page 316.

Answer on page 316.

Answer on page 316.

Answer on page 316.

Answer on page 317.

Answer on page 317.

Answer on page 317.

Answer on page 317.

Answer on page 318.

Answer on page 318.

Answer on page 318.

Answer on page 318.

Answer on page 319.

Answer on page 319.

Answer on page 319.

Answer on page 319.

Answer on page 320.

Answer on page 320.

Answer on page 320.

Answer on page 320.

Answer on page 321.

Answer on page 321.

Answer on page 321.

Answer on page 321.

Answer on page 322.

Answer on page 322.

Answer on page 322.

Answer on page 322.

Answer on page 323.

Answer on page 323.

Answer on page 323.

Answer on page 323.

Answer on page 324.

Answer on page 324.

Answer on page 324.

Answer on page 324.

Answer on page 325.

Answer on page 325.

Answer on page 325.

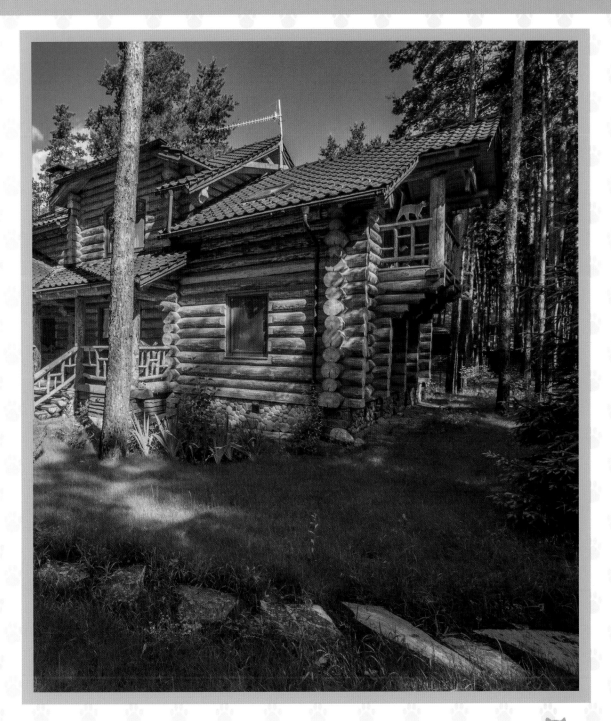

Answer on page 325.

Answer on page 326.

Answer on page 326.

Answer on page 326.

Answer on page 326.

Answer on page 327.

Answer on page 327.

Answer on page 327.

Answer on page 327.

Answer on page 328.

Answer on page 328.

Answer on page 328.

Answer on page 328.

Answer on page 329.

Answer on page 329.

Answer on page 329.

Answer on page 329.

Answer on page 330.

Answer on page 330.

Answer on page 330.

Answer on page 330.

Answer on page 331.

Answer on page 331.

Answer on page 331.

Answer on page 331.

Answer on page 332.

Answer on page 332.

Answer on page 332.

Answer on page 332.

Answer on page 333.

Answer on page 333.

Answer on page 333.

Answer on page 333.

Answer on page 334.

Answer on page 334.

Answer on page 334.

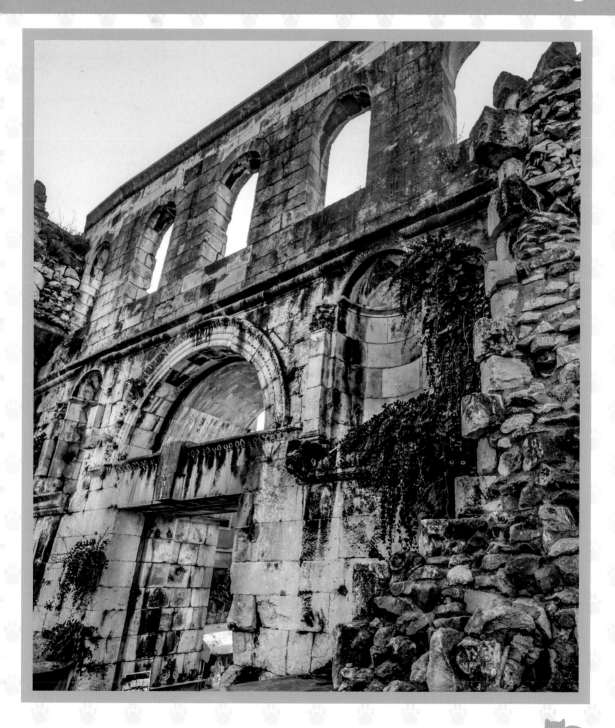

Answer on page 334.

Answer on page 335.

Answer on page 335.

Answer on page 335.

Answer on page 335.

Answer on page 336.

Answer on page 336.

Answer on page 336.

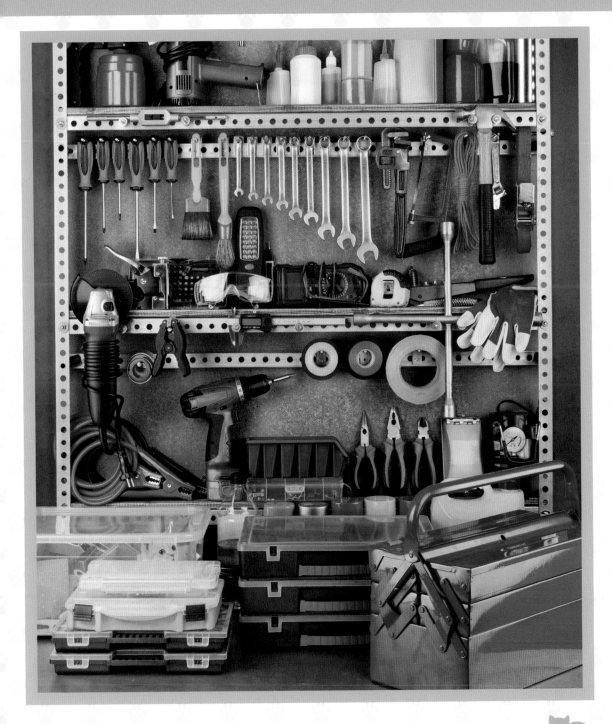

Answer on page 336.

Answer on page 337.

Answer on page 337.

Answer on page 337.

Answer on page 337.

Answer on page 338.

Answer on page 338.

Answer on page 338.

Answer on page 338.

Answer on page 339.

Answer on page 339.

Answer on page 339.

Answer on page 339.

Answer on page 340.

Answer on page 340.

Answer on page 340.

Answer on page 340.

Answer on page 341.

Answer on page 341.

Answer on page 341.

Answer on page 341.

Answer on page 342.

Answer on page 342.

Answer on page 342.

Answer on page 342.

Answer on page 343.

Answer on page 343.

Answer on page 343.

Answer on page 343.

Answer on page 344.

Answer on page 344.

Answer on page 344.

Answer on page 344.

Answer on page 345.

Answer on page 345.

Answer on page 345.

Answer on page 345.

Answer on page 346.

Answer on page 346.

Answer on page 346.

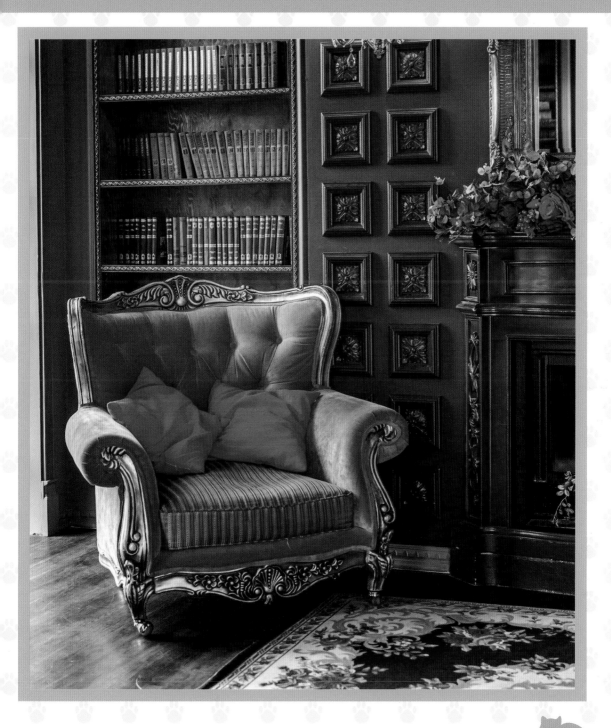

Answer on page 346.

Answer on page 347.

Answer on page 347.

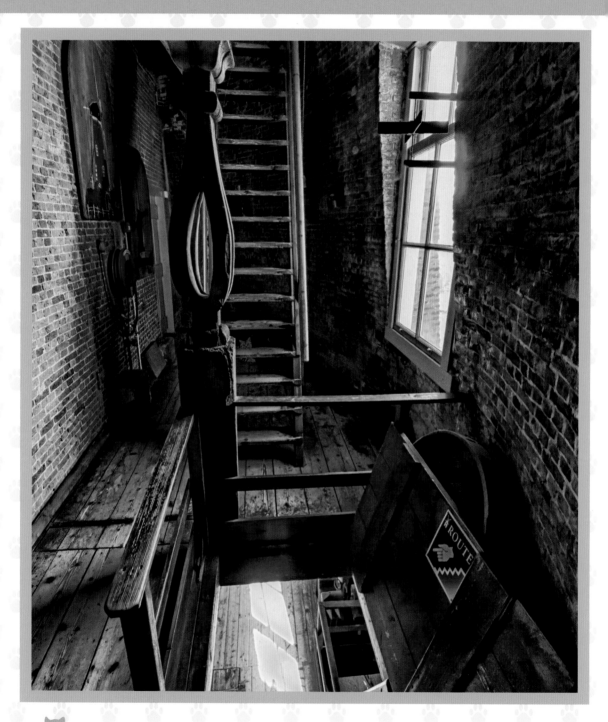

Answer on page 347.

Answer on page 347.

Answer on page 348.

Answer on page 348.

Answer on page 348.

Answer on page 348.

Answer on page 349.

Answer on page 349.

Answer on page 349.

Answer on page 349.

Answer on page 350.

Answer on page 350.

Answer on page 350.

Answer on page 350.

Answer on page 351.

Answer on page 351.

Answer on page 351.

Answer on page 351.

Answer on page 352.

Answer on page 352.

Answer on page 352.

Answer on page 352.

Answer on page 353.

Answer on page 353.

Answer on page 353.

Answer on page 353.

Answer on page 354.

Answer on page 354.

Answer on page 354.

Answer on page 354.

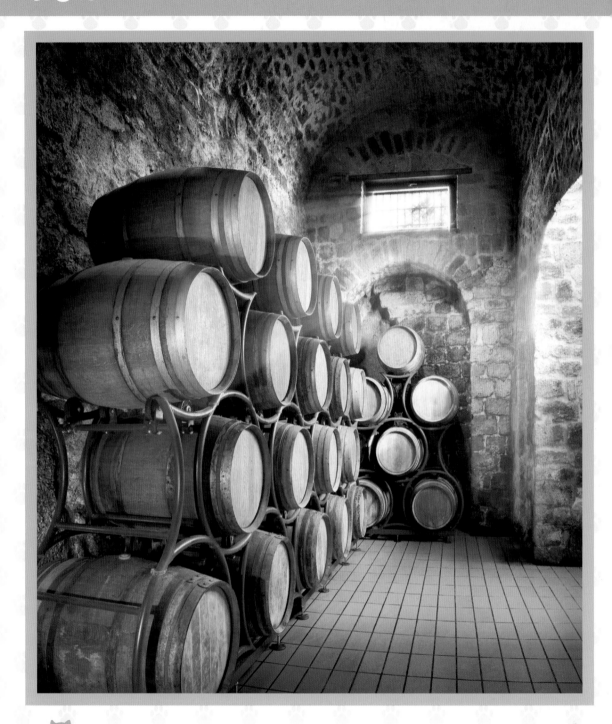

Answer on page 355.

Answer on page 355.

Answer on page 355.

Answer on page 355.

Answer on page 356.

Answer on page 356.

Answer on page 356.

Answer on page 356.

Answer on page 357.

Answer on page 357.

Answer on page 357.

Answer on page 357.

Answer on page 358.

Answer on page 358.

Answer on page 358.

Answer on page 358.

Answer on page 359.

Answer on page 359.

Answer on page 359.

Answer on page 359.

211

Answer on page 360.

Answer on page 360.

Answer on page 360.

Answer on page 360.

Answer on page 361.

Answer on page 361.

Answer on page 361.

Answer on page 361.

Answer on page 362.

Answer on page 362.

Answer on page 362.

Answer on page 362.

Answer on page 363.

Answer on page 363.

Answer on page 363.

ON THE BOAT

Answer on page 363.

Answer on page 364.

Answer on page 364.

Answer on page 364.

Answer on page 364.

Answer on page 365.

Answer on page 365.

Answer on page 365.

Answer on page 365.

Answer on page 366.

Answer on page 366.

Answer on page 366.

Answer on page 366.

Answer on page 367.

Answer on page 367.

Answer on page 367.

Answer on page 367.

Answer on page 368.

Answer on page 368.

Answer on page 368.

Answer on page 368.

Answer on page 369.

Answer on page 369.

Answer on page 369.

Answer on page 369.

Answer on page 370.

Answer on page 370.

Answer on page 370.

Answer on page 370.

Answer on page 371.

Answer on page 371.

Answer on page 371.

Answer on page 371.

Answer on page 372.

Answer on page 372.

Answer on page 372.

Answer on page 372.

Answer on page 373.

Answer on page 373.

Answer on page 373.

Answer on page 373.

Answer on page 374.

Answer on page 374.

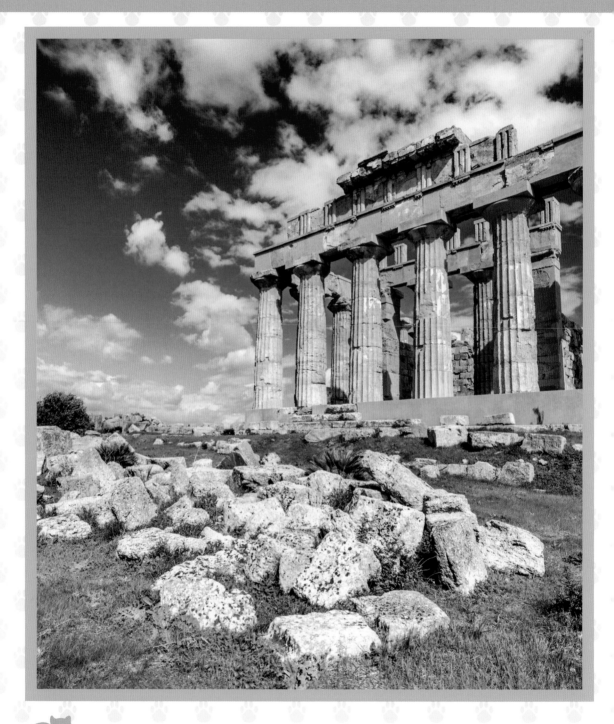

Answer on page 374.

Answer on page 374.

Answer on page 375.

Answer on page 375.

Answer on page 375.

Answer on page 375.

Answer on page 376.

Answer on page 376.

Answer on page 376.

Answer on page 376.

Answer on page 377.

Answer on page 377.

Answer on page 377.

Answer on page 377.

Answer on page 378.

Answer on page 378.

Answer on page 378.

Answer on page 378.

Answer on page 379.

Answer on page 379.

Answer on page 379.

Answer on page 379.

Answer on page 380.

Answer on page 380.

Answer on page 380.

Answer on page 381.

Answer on page 381.

Answer on page 381.

Answer on page 382.

Answer on page 382.

Answer on page 382.

Answer on page 383.

Answer on page 383.

Answer on page 383.

Answer on page 384.

Answer on page 384.

Answer on page 384.

Answer on page 384.

Answer Key

1 (page 4)

3 (page 6)

2 (page 5)

4 (page 7)

Answer Key

5 (page 8)

7 (page 10)

6 (page 9)

8 (page 11)

Answer Key

9 (page 12)

11 (page 14)

10 (page 13)

12 (page 15)

Answer Key

13 (page 16)

15 (page 18)

14 (page 17)

16 (page 19)

Answer Key

17 (page 20)

18 (page 21)

19 (page 22)

20 (page 23)

Answer Key

21 (page 24)

23 (page 26)

22 (page 25)

24 (page 27)

Answer Key

25 (page 28)

27 (page 30)

26 (page 29)

28 (page 31)

Answer Key

29 (page 32)

31 (page 34)

30 (page 33)

32 (page 35)

Answer Key

33 (page 36)

35 (page 38)

34 (page 37)

36 (page 39)

Answer Key

37 (page 40)

39 (page 42)

38 (page 41)

40 (page 43)

Answer Key

41 (page 44)

43 (page 46)

42 (page 45)

44 (page 47)

Answer Key

45 (page 48)

47 (page 50)

46 (page 49)

48 (page 51)

Answer Key

49 (page 52)

51 (page 54)

50 (page 53)

52 (page 55)

Answer Key

53 (page 56)

55 (page 58)

54 (page 57)

56 (page 59)

Answer Key

57 (page 60)

59 (page 62)

58 (page 61)

60 (page 63)

Answer Key

61 (page 64)

63 (page 66)

62 (page 65)

64 (page 67)

Answer Key

65 (page 68)

67 (page 70)

66 (page 69)

68 (page 71)

Answer Key

69 (page 72)

71 (page 74)

70 (page 73)

72 (page 75)

Answer Key

73 (page 76)

75 (page 78)

74 (page 77)

76 (page 79)

Answer Key

77 (page 80)

79 (page 82)

78 (page 81)

80 (page 83)

Answer Key

81 (page 84)

82 (page 85)

83 (page 86)

84 (page 87)

Answer Key

85 (page 88)

87 (page 90)

86 (page 89)

88 (page 91)

Answer Key

89 (page 92)

91 (page 94)

90 (page 93)

92 (page 95)

Answer Key

93 (page 96)

94 (page 97)

95 (page 98)

96 (page 99)

Answer Key

97 (page 100)

99 (page 102)

98 (page 101)

100 (page 103)

Answer Key

101 (page 104)

102 (page 105)

103 (page 106)

104 (page 107)

Answer Key

105 (page 108)

106 (page 109)

107 (page 110)

108 (page 111)

Answer Key

109 (page 112)

111 (page 114)

110 (page 113)

112 (page 115)

Answer Key

113 (page 116)

115 (page 118)

114 (page 117)

116 (page 119)

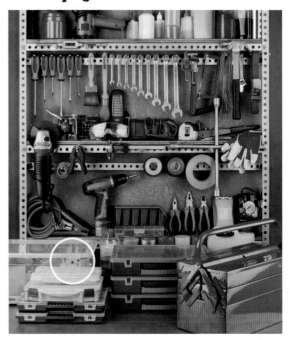

Answer Key

117 (page 120)

119 (page 122)

118 (page 121)

120 (page 123)

Answer Key

121 (page 124)

123 (page 126)

122 (page 125)

124 (page 127)

Answer Key

125 (page 128)

127 (page 130)

126 (page 129)

128 (page 131)

Answer Key

129 (page 132)

131 (page 134)

130 (page 133)

132 (page 135)

Answer Key

133 (page 136)

135 (page 138)

134 (page 137)

136 (page 139)

Answer Key

137 (page 140)

139 (page 142)

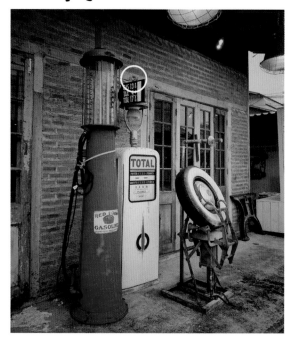

138 (page 141)

140 (page 143)

Answer Key

141 (page 144)

143 (page 146)

142 (page 145)

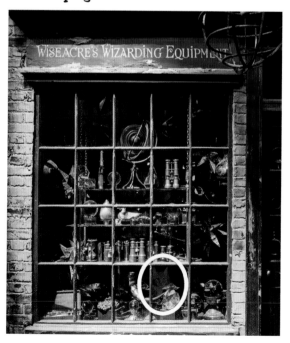

144 (page 147)

Answer Key

145 (page 148)

147 (page 150)

146 (page 149)

148 (page 151)

Answer Key

149 (page 152)

151 (page 154)

150 (page 153)

152 (page 155)

Answer Key

153 (page 156)

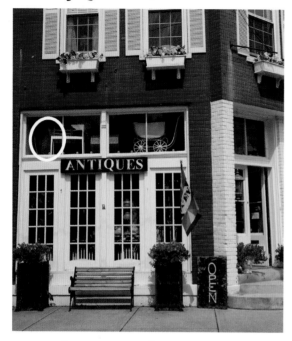

155 (page 158)

154 (page 157)

156 (page 159)

Answer Key

157 (page 160)

159 (page 162)

158 (page 161)

160 (page 163)

Answer Key

161 (page 164)

163 (page 166)

162 (page 165)

164 (page 167)

Answer Key

165 (page 168)

167 (page 170)

166 (page 169)

168 (page 171)

Answer Key

169 (page 172)

171 (page 174)

170 (page 173)

172 (page 175)

Answer Key

173 (page 176)

175 (page 178)

174 (page 177)

176 (page 179)

Answer Key

177 (page 180)

179 (page 182)

178 (page 181)

180 (page 183)

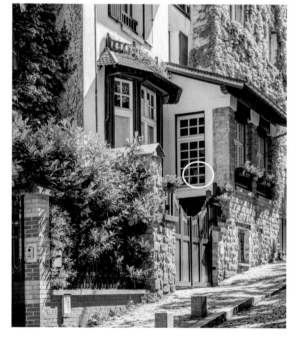

Answer Key

181 (page 184)

183 (page 186)

182 (page 185)

184 (page 187)

Answer Key

185 (page 188)

187 (page 190)

186 (page 189)

188 (page 191)

Answer Key

189 (page 192)

191 (page 194)

190 (page 193)

192 (page 195)

Answer Key

193 (page 196)

194 (page 197)

195 (page 198)

196 (page 199)

Answer Key

197 (page 200)

199 (page 202)

198 (page 201)

200 (page 203)

Answer Key

201 (page 204)

203 (page 206)

202 (page 205)

204 (page 207)

Answer Key

205 (page 208)

207 (page 210)

206 (page 209)

208 (page 211)

Answer Key

209 (page 212)

211 (page 214)

210 (page 213)

212 (page 215)

Answer Key

213 (page 216)

215 (page 218)

214 (page 217)

216 (page 219)

Answer Key

217 (page 220)

219 (page 222)

218 (page 221)

220 (page 223)

Answer Key

221 (page 224)

223 (page 226)

222 (page 225)

224 (page 227)

Answer Key

225 (page 228)

227 (page 230)

226 (page 229)

228 (page 231)

Answer Key

229 (page 232)

231 (page 234)

230 (page 233)

232 (page 235)

Answer Key

233 (page 236)

235 (page 238)

234 (page 237)

236 (page 239)

Answer Key

237 (page 240)

239 (page 242)

238 (page 241)

240 (page 243)

Answer Key

241 (page 244)

243 (page 246)

242 (page 245)

244 (page 247)

Answer Key

245 (page 248)

247 (page 250)

246 (page 249)

248 (page 251)

Answer Key

249 (page 252)

251 (page 254)

250 (page 253)

252 (page 255)

Answer Key

253 (page 256)

254 (page 257)

255 (page 258)

256 (page 259)

Answer Key

257 (page 260)

259 (page 262)

258 (page 261)

260 (page 263)

Answer Key

261 (page 264)

263 (page 266)

262 (page 265)

264 (page 267)

Answer Key

265 (page 268)

267 (page 270)

266 (page 269)

268 (page 271)

Answer Key

269 (page 272)

271 (page 274)

270 (page 273)

272 (page 275)

Answer Key

273 (page 276)

275 (page 278)

274 (page 277)

276 (page 279)

Answer Key

277 (page 280)

279 (page 282)

278 (page 281)

280 (page 283)

Answer Key

281 (page 284)

283 (page 286)

282 (page 285)

284 (page 287)

Answer Key

285 (page 288)

287 (page 290)

286 (page 289)

288 (page 291)

Answer Key

289 (page 292)

290 (page 293)

291 (page 294)

Answer Key

292 (page 295)

293 (page 296)

294 (page 297)

Answer Key

296 (page 299)

295 (page 298)

297 (page 300)

Answer Key

298 (page 301)

300 (page 303)

299 (page 302)

Answer Key

301 (page 304)

303 (page 306)

302 (page 305)

304 (page 307)